Haybox C

Save Energy with Thermal Cooking

Jane & Seggy Segaran

First published in 2017 by Ohm Books Publishing, UK

This 3rd edition published September 2020

© 2020 Jane & Seggy Segaran

All rights reserved. This publication may be reproduced, stored or transmitted, in any form or by any means, only with the prior permission in writing of the author, or in the case of reprographic reproduction in accordance with the terms of licences issued by the Copyright Licensing Agency. Enquiries concerning reproduction outside those terms should be sent to the author at the address below.

9, The Pastures
York
YO24 2JE
UK

ISBN: 9798683748104

CONTENTS

	Page
Introduction	5
Advantages of haybox cooking	7
Guidelines for use	10
Food safety	12
Cooking times for basic items	14
Five Homemade Haybox Cookers	16
Commercial haybox cookers	25
Haybox vs. Slow Cookers	28
A meal cooked on a single fire	29
Making Bread	31
Yoghurt in a Haybox	32
Cooking for one	33
Integrated Cooking	35
Recipes	38
Autumn Fruit Compote	40
Bean and Coconut Stew	41
Boston Baked Beans	42
Black Beans and Rice	43
Dhal Masala	45
Kale and Potato Soup	45
Mexican Beans	46
Poached Fruit	47
Potato, Spinach and Lentil Curry	48
Quorn Curry	49
Ratatouille	50
Simple Mixed Rice	51
Spicy Lentil and Carrot Soup	53
Vegetable Tagine	54
Very Easy and Delicious Bean Stew	55
Appendix	
Plans for the Haybox Cooker Stool	56

Introduction

What is a haybox? It's basically an insulated box or bag in which you place your partly cooked food. The heat energy held in the pot and the food completes the cooking process without any external heat input.

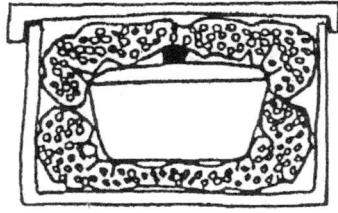 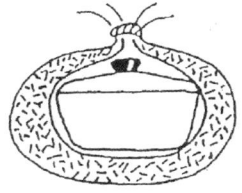

We first came across haybox cooking a few years ago when researching fuel saving cooking methods. Having tried it out a few times we were hooked. The idea of preparing a couple of dishes and then putting it into a haybox while we popped out for a few hours was quite attractive. We would then come back to a steaming hot meal that was perfectly cooked with no risk of burning. It surprised us that even after 3 or 4 hours we needed oven gloves to handle the cooking pots as they were still very hot.

Haybox cookers are so called because the early versions used hay as insulation. It is also referred to as thermal, fireless or retained heat cooking. In this book we will continue to use the term haybox cooking.

Haybox cooking was first recorded as being used in the early 19th century with the inventor Karl von Drais being credited with coming up with a novel design. They were used during the Second World War to conserve precious fuel.

Various forms of haybox cookers are used widely in the developing world to cut down on the use of firewood. This saves time spent in gathering fuel and helps reduce deforestation. Conservative estimates of fuel saving vary from 40 - 50 %.

The purpose of this book is to promote the use of haybox cooking to a wide audience. Many different designs are presented as well as recipes and advise on cooking times.

We have really enjoyed working on this book. We hope that the reader catches the haybox cooking bug and the many benefits it can bring.

Jane and Seggy Segaran

Advantages of Haybox Cooking

Cooking with a haybox needs more planning than conventional cooking. They also cannot be used for high temperature cooking such as baking or frying. However there are many advantages to using haybox cookers for day to day cooking.

Fuel saving: Using a haybox can easily save up to 50% of the energy required to cook food. This is because instead of the heat from a saucepan being lost it is trapped by the insulation and used to heat and cook the food. The energy saving is the same whether it is gas, electricity, wood or charcoal. For low income families in developing countries that have to buy firewood this can make a significant difference.

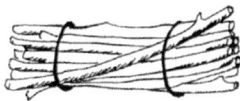   Less firewood

   Less money

Tasty, nutritious food: The slow cooking in a haybox retains much of the flavours and nutrients in food.

No risk of burning food: When cooking on a fire, sometimes food needs to be left to simmer on a low heat. This has to be frequently checked and the food stirred to prevent burning at the bottom. With a haybox, the heat is directed to the pot from all sides and there is absolutely no risk of burning. The food can be left unattended till it is needed.

Reduce water usage: When food is simmered on a fire a lot of water is boiled away. However, when cooking with a haybox the water in the pot is retained and less water can be used. For example one uses two cups of water to a cup of rice when cooking on a fire. With a haybox this can be reduced to one a half cups of water to a cup of rice.

Only one fire needed: When cooking a variety of food (e.g. potatoes, vegetables and meat) on a stove top, at least three fires are needed. With a haybox this can be done with a single fire. Each item can be brought to the boil and then placed in the haybox, freeing up the flame for the next dish.

Convenience: With food left cooking in a haybox, there is no need to reheat food – it is ready steaming hot when you need it. It works like a slow cooker without an external heat input.

Reduces smoke inhalation: In many developing countries, open fires are used for cooking food by low income families. The smoke from these fires has been shown to result in many breathing related diseases. Using a haybox means less time spent leaning over a smoking fire and reduces this risk.

Guidelines for use

A well constructed haybox can keep food temperatures well above 65 deg C after 3 hours. There are a number of factors that determine the effectiveness of a haybox.

Insulation: The thickness of the insulation is very important to the working of the haybox cooker. If kapok, polystyrene or cork is used, this must be at least 5 cm (2 inches) thick all round the pot. If straw, newspaper, cotton or chaff is used as insulation then it is good to aim for a thickness of around 10 cm (4 inches).

Thickness of pot: A thicker walled pot works better than a thinner one as it retains more heat. This will then slowly release heat while in the haybox and help cook the food and keep it hot for longer.

Use pot with lid

Lid: It's important to have a tight fitting lid on the pot to reduce evaporation and heat loss. One can also wrap the pot in a towel before putting it into the haybox – this will help keep the lid on tight. When heating the ingredients up before putting it in the haybox make sure the lid is on the pot. This way the lid heats up to the same temperature as the pot. Putting a cold lid on a heated pot will lower the overall temperature.

Amount of food in pot: The pot needs to be at least 3/4 full of food to ensure that the food temperature remains above 70 deg C after 3 hours. If the pot is only a 1/4 full then after 3 hours the temperature could be as low as 55 deg C and the food will need to be heated up before eating.

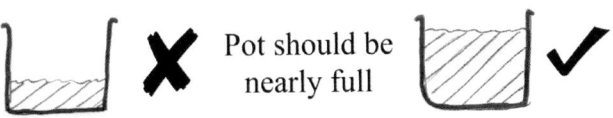
Pot should be nearly full

The table below shows the difference between a haybox cooker made to the above guidelines and a poorly constructed one. After three hours the temperature difference could be as much as 16 deg C.

Elapsed time	Nearly full pot and well made	Quarter full pot and poorly made
1 hour	90 deg C	84 deg C
2 hours	79 deg C	65 deg C
3 hours	70 deg C	54 deg C

Checking on the food: Fight the temptation to keep checking the food. Every time the lid is opened heat will escape from the pot thus slowing down the cooking process. Just trust the cooking process and leave things to cook in the retained heat.

Food Safety

One of the main concerns when cooking food in a haybox is the growth of bacteria in food kept warm for a long time. The graph below shows the food safety advice for the UK. The safety advice in other countries is very similar.

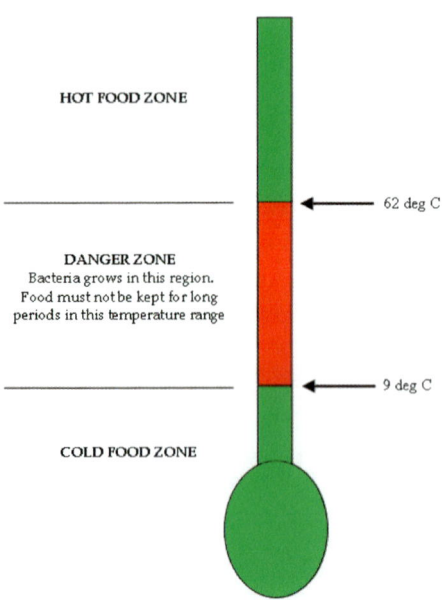

When food is heated above 70 deg C the micro-organisms are deactivated. As the food in the haybox cools, and the temperature drops below 62 deg C, there is a risk that these will start growing again.

In a well constructed haybox, the time for the temperature to drop to 65 deg C is more than 3 hours. It will take a further 2 hours for the temperature to drop to 55 deg C. The risk of significant bacterial growth is negligible and the food should still be safe as long as it is consumed straight away.

The advice from the Apprevecho Research Centre on food safety when cooking in a haybox is:

"Bacterial poisoning can be avoided by two simple steps. Make sure that the food is initially boiled for at least 5 minutes. Then keep the lid closed from that point on and re-heat meat dishes before serving."

In general, food can be cooked in the haybox for up to 5 hours and then eaten without having to be re-heated. At above 55 deg C it should still be considered hot. Make sure to keep the lid on till the food is brought to the table and consume it straight away.

While experimenting and getting familiar with haybox cooking, a thermometer will very useful. The one below has a long lead which allows the probe to be immersed in the food while the display can be kept on top of the cooker.

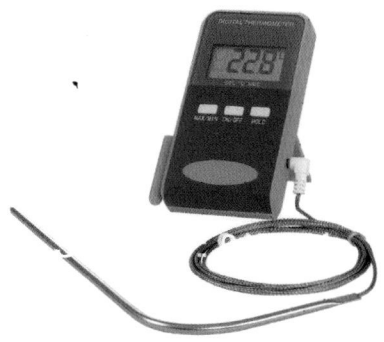

Cooking times for basic items

Using a haybox is just like using any other type of cooker. A good cook will learn from experience and adjust their cooking to suit the type of haybox that they are using.

Rice

Wash the rice. Add 1.5 measures of water to a measure of rice. Bring to boil on a fire in a suitable pot with the lid on. Bring off the fire and place in the haybox. The rice will be cooked perfectly in an hour but will keep hot for up to 5 hours.

Potatoes

Scrub potatoes. If mashing, then peel otherwise leave skin on. Cut into roughly egg-sized pieces. Cover with water and bring to the boil. Remove from fire and place in the haybox. The potatoes will be cooked in an hour and will keep hot for up to 5 hours.

Dried beans and chickpeas

Soak overnight. Drain and cover with water. Bring to boil in a pan with a lid. Roll boil for 10 minutes. Remove from fire and place in haybox. They will be cooked in around 3 hours.

Five Homemade Haybox Cookers

When promoting any product or technique, it's important to adopt it and try it out yourself. Having come across Haybox cooking and keen to promote it in Rwanda we made and tried out our first one. Since then we have made various haybox cookers – here are details on 5 of them.

Haybox made from a plastic storage crate

Here you can see a very simple Haybox made with items we had round the house. Towels, sleeping bag and a storage crate. This could hold 2 pots side by side. The first picture below show the items used and the second one shows the sleeping bag spread out to line the inside of the crate.

The towels are useful in holding the pot and lid together, providing extra insulation as well as serving as oven gloves. This storage crate is big enough to hold two pots side by side – in our case mostly one with rice and the other with a curry.

The towels also protect the sleeping bag from spills and cooking odours. It's necessary to wash the towels from time to time to freshen them up. The final stage is to wrap the sleeping bag around the top of the pots before popping the lid on.

We use this type of haybox a lot of the time for convenience. It allows you to cook up to 3 hours before mealtimes and have the food served hot when it is needed. The latest dish to be cooked in this haybox was a bean stew that was prepared at home around 5 o'clock and then taken in the haybox by car to a fund-raising meal that was served at 7.30 pm.

Wicker Basket Haybox Cooker

This design of haybox is popular in East Africa where it is generally referred to as fireless cooking rather than as haybox. You will need a large wicker basket, some colourful material and kapok or other insulating material. We cut up an old sleeping bag for this. Thanks to Bernhard Muller for the design (we have varied it a little from the original).

We lined the base of the basket with the insulation from the cut up sleeping bag. Lots of pieces of the sleeping bag were placed around the sides of the basket using the pot placed in the middle as a guide.

A large piece of the colourful cloth was placed on top of this with the cooking pot sat in the middle. Excess cloth was trimmed off and the basket finished off with a large black ribbon tied onto the outside over the cloth. The cushion to go on top was made with the same material.

The finished wicker basket haybox cooker is shown below. It was fun to make and looks good in any kitchen. We often put a weight on top of the cushion to keep it on and show others that it's in use.

The Haybox Stool

This is our favourite as it doubles up as a stool. Many a time we have surprised guests by asking them to get off this to fish out a dish cooked hours ago. The cooker enclosure is made of wood and the insulation is provided by 2 large cushions stuffed with crushed up newspaper. There are a few pictures overleaf to show this cooker.

Haybox Cooking

The Wonderbox

This was the name of a haybox cooker sold in Southern Africa many years ago. It is basically a cardboard box with 2 cushions inside. We have recreated this design as a flat packed version that can be taken to workshops and festivals. All that is needed to complete the cooker is some insulation. The parts that make this up and the finished version are shown below.

One cushion is very large (100 x 75 cm). This is half filled with insulation and the bottom two corners pinned together to form a flat base as shown overleaf.

Haybox Cooking

The top of the cushion is gathered and place it in the cardboard box pushing the gathered part right into the insulation to make room for a pot.

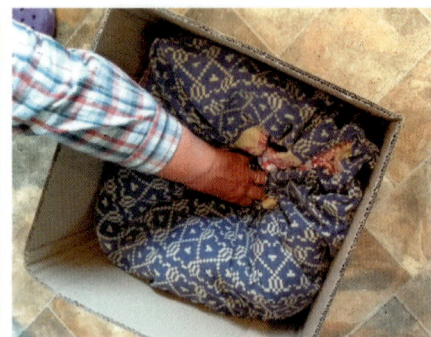

Once the small cushion (50 x 50 cm) is filled with insulation, the Wonderbox is ready for use. When the pot of food is boiling pop this into the well made in the big cushion, place the small cushion on top and finish off with the lid. Couple of hours later your food will be ready cooked and piping hot.

Haybox Cooking

Tip: The cardboard box can be taped up, but an old trick is to use the flaps as shown below to secure it.

Kitchen Drawer Haybox Cooker

This is the simplest one we have ever used. Simply add a large cushion to the base of a deep drawer, add the pot and a cushion on top. Like in the storage crate cooker, one can easily use an old sleeping bag and a towel as insulation around the pot. The pictures below use the same cushions as the Wonderbox cooker.

Haybox Cooking

Commercial haybox cookers

For those who would rather buy a haybox cooker than make one, there are some available commercially.

The Wonderbag

This is probably the best known commercially available haybox. It was designed in South Africa and is widely used there and in many other African countries.

The cooking pot is placed in the large insulated bag and the smaller cushion placed on top. The drawstring is pulled tight and the food is then left to cook.

The Wonderbag comes in a variety of lovely colours and in two sizes. It uses polystyrene beads for insulation. Prices are from £35 to £45 dependent on size.

Vacuum Thermal Insulation Cooker

This device looks like a slow cooker but does not use any power. The insulation is provided by a vacuum, similar to those used in thermos flasks.

The food is cooked in the inner pot and then transferred to the vacuum cooker to continue cooking with retained heat.

The model shown here is manufactured in Japan and is available in the UK for around £200.

The Wonderbox Thermal Cooker

This haybox cooker is based on one that was designed and supplied in Southern Africa. It is supplied as a self-assembly kit and consists of a custom made cardboard box, lid and cushion covers. The cardboard is of a double wall construction, making it very durable.

This is made in the UK and is available from on-line outlets like Amazon for around £20. It is supplied as a kit – all the user has to do is to fill the 2 cushions with suitable insulation,

Haybox vs Slow Cooker

Cooking in a haybox is similar to using a slow cooker but there are some important differences. The main advantage of a slow cooker is that it can cook food over a long period, say up 6 to 8 hours and the food still stays piping hot. However the haybox does have the following advantages.

- A haybox does not need any power after the food is initially heated up. This means that as well saving energy it can be used in places without access to electricity. It is a great accessory to take camping or in a caravan.

- A slow cooker is normally left on a timer, so you need to stick to your plans – otherwise the food can dry out or burn. With a haybox, if you are delayed then simply reheat on your return – there is no risk of your food burning.

- Food cooking in a haybox is entirely portable. It can be put in the back of a car and delivered to someone working outside as a piping hot meal up to 3 or 4 hours later.

- When preparing food just using one stove, the haybox is an essential accessory. Once a dish is initially heated up it can be left to cook in the haybox while the stove is used to prepare further dishes.

A meal cooked on a single fire

One of the major benefits with haybox cooking is that it makes it easy to cook with just one flame. One can partly cook each dish in turn and then place it in a haybox, moving on to the next dish. As well as saving on fuel, this will also result in a huge time saving, reducing the cooking time for 3 dishes from 2 to 3 hours to just over an hour. This is because instead of standing over the fire, all the simmering is done in the haybox without using any fuel.

Prior to our trip to Sri Lanka in 2019, we decided to give this a try. The only way to promote new ways of doing things is to use it all the time yourself.

The meal we decided to cook was rice, dhal and Brinjal curry. Each dish had approximately 20 minutes on the fire bringing it up to temperature and then placed in a haybox. Two hours later it was all cooked and ready to eat.

Here are the 3 haybox cookers used for this meal and the results.

This meal took us a total of 1 hour to prepare and was piping hot when we ate more than 2 hours later. Without the haybox cookers, it would have taken nearly 2 hours to prepare on a single fire and would have used twice the amount of fuel.

Making Bread without an Oven

For this we used recycled soup tins - the ring pull kind to avoid cut fingers. They were half filled (to allow room for rising) with quick rise bread dough and covered securely with tin foil. They were then boiled up in a pan of water with the lid on for 8 minutes. Too much water can cause the tins to float! The pan with the tins still immersed in water was wrapped in a towel and placed in the haybox cooker and left for 4 hours. Below are some photos from this trial.

The finished bread is more steamed than baked but none the less quite delicious! They were nice toasted and tasted a bit like muffins. This is a great way to make bread if you are living off-grid or cannot afford an oven.

Quick Rise Bread Dough Recipe

500g strong bread flour
2 teaspoons salt
2 teaspoons sugar
3 ½ teaspoons active baking yeast
Warm water to mix

Yoghurt in a Haybox

3 tablespoons live yoghurt
1 pint milk

Heat milk to 85 deg C
Cool to 45 deg C
Mix in yoghurt
Pour into jam jars and seal
Pop into haybox, cover with hot-water bottle
and wrap both in a towel.
Put the cushion on top and close the lid
Leave overnight

The yoghurt will be ready in the morning.

Cooking for one

Haybox cooking is ideal when cooking for families as this usually involves large pots filled full of food. There is a lot of heat in these when placed inside a haybox cooker and this results in well cooked piping hot food.

When dealing with smaller quantities of food, one option is to place two small pots inside the same haybox cooker. The combined heat from the two pots with the food will give the same result as cooking in a larger pot.

Another solution when cooking small quantities is to use a hot water bottle filled with boiling water underneath the cooking pot. The heat from this will help cook the food by keeping the temperature high.

 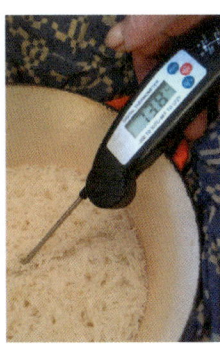 

In this cooking session where a small amount of rice was cooked the temperature was as follows. The rice was cooked perfectly.

After 5 minutes   94 deg C
After 2 hours   75 deg C
After 3.5 hours   64 deg C

In the above cooking session, we used a 3 litre pot with a small quantity of rice and a hot water bottle. If a 1 litre cast aluminium pot is used then one could dispense with the hot water bottle and just cook conventionally with the haybox cooker.

We keep a range of pots and choose the one that is the right size for the amount of food that we are cooking. The black pot is 25 cm wide and holds 4 litres while the blue pot is 21 cm wide and holds 2 litres. We use the red pot when cooking small quantities – it's 17 cm wide and holds just 1 litre.

Integrated Cooking

While haybox cooking can save around 50% of fuel compared to normal cooking, when it is combined with other forms of low impact cooking the savings can increase to 70 to 80%. Examples of this are when it is combined with the use of Rocket Stoves or Solar Cooking. Food cooked by either of these methods can be transferred to a haybox cooker to carry on cooking and keep warm for many hours.

Rocket Stoves

A rocket stove is a clean and efficient cooking stove using wood fuel which is burnt in a high-temperature combustion chamber containing an insulated vertical chimney. This ensures complete combustion before the flames reach the cooking surface.

Here are the key design principles of a Rocket Stove.

1. Insulate around the fire using lightweight, heat-resistant materials.
2. Place an insulated short chimney right above the fire to burn up the smoke and speed up the draft.
3. Heat and burn the tips of the sticks as they enter the fire to make flame, not smoke.
4. High and low heat is created by how many sticks are pushed into the fire.
5. Maintain a good fast draft from under the fire, up through the coals. Avoid allowing too much extra air in above the fire to cool it.
6. Too little draft being pulled into the fire will

result in smoke and excess charcoal.
7. Keep unrestricted airflow by maintaining constant cross sectional area through the stove. The opening into the fire, the size of the spaces within the stove through which hot air flows, and the chimney should all be about the same size.
8. Use a grate under the fire. ` Insulate the heat flow path, from the fire, to and around the pot(s) or griddle.
9. Maximize heat transfer to the pot with properly sized gaps.

Here is a drawing of the main features of the stove.

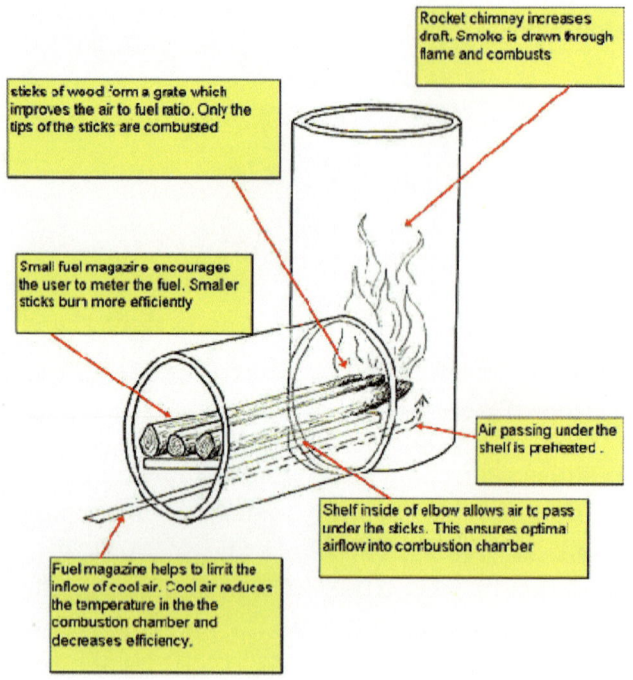

Haybox Cooking 36

Solar Cooking

Solar cookers use the power of the sun to cook food directly. A typical design is shown below. The heat from the sun is trapped in an insulated box behind a sheet of glass. Additional reflectors can be used to collect heat from a larger area. The food is cooked in a black pot which converts the radiated energy from the sun into heat. A black metal sheet at the base of the cooker is used to retain the heat.

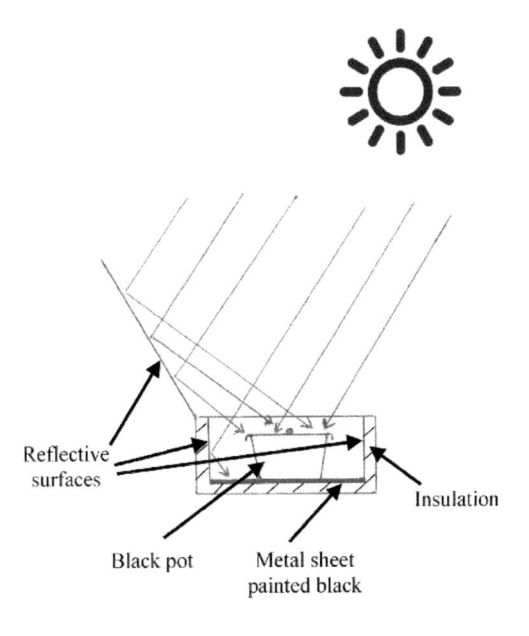

Food takes longer to cook in a Solar Cooker, when compared to conventional cooking. For example, rice will take around 2 hours. However it provides a way of cooking food which does not use any fuel nor cost any money.

Recipes

We have presented a few tasty recipes here for you to try with your haybox cooker. They all happen to be vegan or vegetarian but can easily be adapted for meat or fish. Once you get a feel for cooking times with the haybox cooker you should feel confident about adapting many normal recipes for cooking in the haybox cooker.

You will get better results by using a cast iron or aluminium pot like the one shown below. It's heavy and will retain more heat. It has a good fitting lid and small handles that don't get in the way of the insulation. Make sure that the pot is almost 3/4s full as this will ensure that the food stays hotter for longer.

When boiling the food before placing in the haybox, make sure that all parts of the food is bubbling and not just the edges in contact with the pot. The lid will need to be on to make sure that it too heats up to the same temperature as the food.

Haybox cookers work best with food that has a large amount of water when cooked like rice, pulses, stews, casseroles, tagines and curries. It also works best with dishes that are normally heated up and then simmered for quite some time on the fire. The fuel needed for simmering is saved by putting the partly cooked food in the haybox cooker and letting the retained heat finish the cooking.

Autumn Fruit Compote

Any combination of fruit is good for this, especially in Autumn when there is a glut of apples, plums and brambles.

2 Apples – peeled, cored and cut into small chunks
500g Plums – halved and stoned
4 oz Brambles
3 tablespoons soft brown sugar (adjust according to taste)

Place the fruit in a pot small enough for the fruit to ¾ fill the pot.
Add 3 tablespoons water and the sugar and stir.
Place the pot on the hob and bring to the boil with the lid on, simmer for 2-3 minutes.
Remove and place in the haybox cooker for 2-3 hours.

Serve with yogurt, ice-cream, cream etc or on top of your breakfast muesli!

Bean and Coconut Stew

I use black beans or butter beans, but any combination of beans is fine for this recipe. I also use any combination of vegetables that happen to be hiding in the pantry. Chop the vegetables fairly small to allow them to cook properly.

1 tablespoon oil
2 onions – chopped
2 garlic cloves – crushed
1 leek
1 pepper
1 courgette
1 aubergine
1 tin beans or 250g of precooked beans
1 tin tomatoes
3 tablespoons molasses
½ can coconut milk or 3 tablespoons coconut powder dissolved in a little hot water
Salt to taste

banana blossom / jack fruit

Cook the onion and garlic in the oil.
Add all the chopped vegetables and continue cooking for around 3 minutes.
Add the coconut milk, salt, molasses and tinned tomatoes. If using whole tomatoes squash down well.
Mix all together and add enough water to cover the stew by 1". Season with salt.
With the lid on the pot bring to the boil and continue boiling for around 8-10 minutes.
Place in the haybox, wrapped in a towel or blanket for 3 hours.
Serve with bread, rice or cous cous.

Boston Baked Beans

2x 235 gm (tinned) haricot beans or pre cooked
1 tin tomatoes squashed
2 large onions – chopped
2 cloves garlic – chopped or crushed
1 tablespoon oil
2 tablespoons black treacle or molasses
2 tablespoons tomato puree
2 teaspoons brown sugar
Salt and Black Pepper

Heat the oil in the saucepan and fry the onions for a few minutes add the garlic and stir.
Add the rest of the ingredients and bring the mixture to the boil adding a little water or stock if necessary. The mixture does not want to have much liquid – so below the level of the beans
Season to taste
Remove from the heat, cover and place in the Haybox.
The dish will be ready after about 2 hours and will keep warm up to 4 hours.

Black Beans and Rice

1 tin (400gm) of black beans
3 tablespoons vegetable oil
1 medium onion - chopped
1 large clove of garlic – chopped or crushed
1 green pepper - chopped
225 gm long grain brown rice
400 ml water
1 teaspoon sea salt
Black pepper

Heat the oil and fry the onion, garlic and pepper for 5 minutes.
Stir in the rice, water, salt, and beans.
Bring to the boil with lid on.
Place in haybox for a minimum of 1 and a half hours.
Add black pepper and salt to taste.

Dhal Masala

1 onion – chopped
2 cloves garlic – chopped or crushed
2 tablespoons oil
2 teaspoons curry powder (more if required)
1 teaspoon turmeric
1 aubergine – cut into 1" chunks
2 sweet peppers – chopped fairly small
½ cup red lentils – washed.
1 tablespoon coconut powder
1 tablespoon tomato puree
Salt to taste

Fry onion and garlic.
Add vegetables and cook for 10 minutes.
Add spices and coconut powder.
Add lentils and enough water to come 2" above the lentils.
Add salt and mix in coconut powder.
Bring to boil with lid on.
Cover and place in haybox for a minimum of 1 hour.
Serve with rice.

Kale and Potato Soup

An adaptation of the Portuguese dish Caldi Verde

4 tablespoons olive oil
2 onions - diced
2 cloves garlic – crushed
300 gms Kale or Cavalo Nero – finely shredded and stalks removed
4 medium potatoes - cubed
Paprika
Salt to taste
1.5 litres Stock

Heat the oil in the pan and fry onion and garlic for 4 minutes to soften.
Stir in the potatoes and cook a further 5 minutes.
Add the Kale and stock and seasoning. Bring to boil with the lid on for 5 minutes. Stir.
Remove from the heat and place in the haybox for at least 1 hour.

Serve with warm bread.

To make a more substantial meal, add chopped pre-cooked veggie sausages to the pan before serving.

Mexican Beans

This needs planning ahead as the beans need to be soaked overnight. Don't add salt until the end as this may stop the beans from cooking.

2 cups black beans
Olive oil
2 onions – chopped
3 sweet peppers – chopped fairly small
3 cloves garlic – crushed
Chopped jalapeno peppers (to your taste!)
1 teaspoon chilli powder
Water or stock
2 tablespoons coconut powder

Soak beans overnight and drain before cooking.

Add oil to pan and sauté onions with garlic for 3 minutes.
Add peppers and cook for a further 3 minutes then add spices and fry for a minute.
Add coconut powder and water to 1 inch above the beans and bring to boil with lid on.
Boil for a further 15 minutes.
Place in haybox to cook for 3 hours. The food will stay warm for up to 5 hours.
Add salt to taste at the end of cooking.
Serve with wraps, salsa and salad.

Poached Fruit

This is a very useful for using up slightly blemished over or under ripe fruit. For this recipe you could use any combination of fruit. It works very well with soft fruit too. Adjust the cooking times slightly as soft fruit would take less time to cook.

3 apples and 3 pears peeled and cored. Chop into 3 cm cubes
1 orange peeled and sliced into rings. Cut the rings in half.
1 tablespoon honey
½ tablespoon brown sugar
A little hot water
2 inch cinnamon stick

Place everything in a small pan, add a little hot water to half way up the fruit.
Bring to boil with lid on.
Place in haybox cooker for 2 hours.

Potato, Spinach and Lentil Curry

2 tbsp of oil
1 onion – chopped
2 cloves garlic – crushed
1 teaspoon mustard seeds
Curry leaves – optional
1 teaspoon chilli powder
1 teaspoon garam masala
1 teaspoon turmeric
1 teaspoon curry powder
4 potatoes – cut into cubes
1 ½ cups red lentils
1 tin chopped tomatoes
300mls water
Salt to taste
Black pepper
1 lb spinach leaves

Heat the oil in a medium sized pan and add mustard seeds and allow to splutter.
Add the chopped onion and garlic and sauté until softening.
Add the curry leaves, and all spices and fry for a minute or two.
Add all the remaining ingredients except the spinach.
Bring to the boil with the lid on.
Add spinach and bring back to boil.
Place in the haybox and leave to cook for 2 hours.
Serve with rice or naan bread.

NOTE: Also delicious using sweet potato instead of potatoes.

Quorn Curry

2 tablespoons oil
2 onions – chopped
2 cloves garlic - crushed
1 aubergine – cut into cubes
2 peppers – cut into cubes
1 bag quorn pieces
2 teaspoons curry powder
1 teaspoon turmeric
1 tablespoon curry paste
2 teaspoons tomato puree
Salt to taste
2 tablespoons coconut milk powder dissolved in a little hot water

Fry onions and garlic in oil for 2 minutes.
Add aubergine, peppers and salt and fry 5 minutes.
Add all remaining ingredients with enough water to cover.
Bring to boil with lid on.
Transfer to fireless cooker and leave to cook for one and a half hours.
Serve with rice or naan bread.

Ratatouille

3 tbsp olive oil
2 onions sliced
3 cloves garlic – crushed
1 aubergine – chopped into 1" cubes
3 courgettes – chopped into 1" cubes
2 peppers – chopped into 1" cubes
½ tin chopped tomatoes or 3 fresh tomatoes chopped
Salt
Black pepper

Heat olive oil in a suitable pot.
Add onions and garlic and fry 5 minutes.
Add all other ingredients and cook 5 – 10 minutes with lid on.
Season to taste.
Place in haybox to cook for one and a half hours.

Simple Mixed Rice

2 tablespoons oil
1 teaspoon mustard seeds
1 clove garlic - crushed
1 onion - chopped
Few spring onions – chopped
Half cup frozen peas
Half cup frozen sweet corn
1 tablespoon curry paste
Salt
1 mug Rice
1 and a half mugs water

Heat oil and splutter mustard seeds.
Add onion and garlic and fry 2 minutes.
Add spring onions and continue cooking for 1 minute.
Add rice, water, corn, peas, salt and curry paste.

Bring to boil with lid on.

Place in haybox for 2 hours. This will stay hot for up to 5 hours.

Spicy Lentil and Carrot Soup

I find this recipe rather more successful if the lentils have been previously cooked. (Cover lentils with boiling water to come 1" above the lentils. Bring to boil with lid on. Place in haybox for 1 hour)

1 Mug Lentils – previously cooked in the haybox.
1 tablespoon oil
2 onions – chopped into fairly small cubes
3 Carrots – Grated
2 tablespoons tomato Puree
Curry powder – to taste
2 cloves garlic – crushed
Salt and black pepper to taste
Stock and hot water

Cook the onion in the oil with the garlic until softening.
Add seasoning, tomato puree and carrot and lentils .
Cook a further 2 minutes.
Pour enough stock and boiling water to come 2"above the lentils.

Bring to boil with the lid on and boil for around 6 minutes.

Place in hay box.
The soup should be ready in two hours.

Vegetable Tagine

2 tablespoons oil
Butternut squash peeled and cut into cubes
2 sweet potatoes peeled and cubes
2 onions –sliced
1 teaspoon turmeric
1 teaspoon jeera
2 teaspoons grated fresh ginger
2 teaspoons cayenne pepper
1 teaspoon ground black pepper
1 teaspoon chilli flakes
Salt to taste
500 mils vegetable stock
1 courgette chopped into cubes
Optional – a handful of dried dates and apricots
Fresh coriander – chopped

Fry the onion and garlic in the oil until softened.
Add all other ingredients and bring to boil with lid on.
Place in the haybox for at least 2 hours.
Garnish with coriander and serve with couscous.

Very Easy and Delicious Bean Stew

(Any combination of tinned beans can be used for this dish)

2 tablespoons oil
3 onions – chopped fairly small
2 cloves garlic - crushed
3 carrots - chopped into small cubes
3 sweet potatoes – peeled and chopped into small cubes
1 leek finely sliced
1 tin Kidney beans
1 tin chick peas
1 tin chopped tomatoes
1 tablespoon curry paste
Salt, black pepper
Stock and boiling water

Cook onion and garlic until softening
Add all the remaining ingredients except the stock, give them a good stir and cook a further 3 minutes.

Pour stock and boiling water to just come to the top of the vegetables.
Season to taste.
Bring to boil with the lid on and boil 8 minutes.

Leave in the haybox for 3 hours.

Serve with chunks of lovely crusty bread.

Appendix: Plans for the Haybox Cooker Stool

Having had such good success with haybox cooking we were keen to design one that would be a permanent fixture in our kitchen. It seemed a good idea to build the haybox as a piece of furniture that was functional. The design below for a haybox stool is our first attempt at this.

Step 1
Build a frame for the stool using 44 x 44 mm smooth planed timber. The 4 vertical pieces were 50 cm long and the 8 horizontal struts were 42 cm long. They were screwed together as shown here. Only 1 screw is used for each joint as the whole structure tightens up when the side panels are fixed.

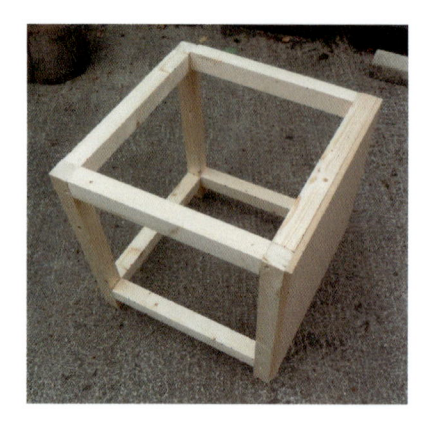

Step 2
Use 12 mm MDF board for the sides. Two of the sides were 50.5 cm (W) x 45 cm (H) and the other two were 53 cm (W) x 45 cm (H). These are shown fixed in the image below. Each side panel was fixed using 4 screws.

Step 3
Use 12 mm MDF board for the base. This is 53 x 53 cm with 4 cut-outs for the legs as shown below. This is held in place by 8 screws, 2 screws each into the four horizontal struts at the base.

Step 4
In this design, we decided to use newspaper as insulation. We made 2 cushions – one of size 90 x 90 cm and the other 80 x 80 cm. We planned to use these

to cover the pot within the stool. The cushions had poppers along one side to allow us to renew the insulation in the future.

Step 5
The lid for the haybox stool is made from 12 mm MDF board 53 x 53 cm in size.

We used 4 wooden blocks as shown below to keep the lid in place. If the cushion pushes up against the lid then clasps may be necessary to fasten the lid firmly onto the box.

The lid was covered with 2 inch thick foam and a piece of plastic table cloth used to cover it. This was stapled to the underside of the lid to hold the foam in place.

We painted the stool haybox a pastel blue shade to match the other colours used in the room. The stool with cover is shown here.

The larger cushion is placed in the stool and a 'nest' made for the pot. This arrangement should be suitable for a variety of sizes of cooking pots.

Stuff the smaller cushion on top of the pot and place or fasten the lid down as required. The stool becomes a useful piece of furniture in the kitchen / dining room.

Printed in Great Britain
by Amazon